Violet Afternoon, 4th edition
© 2021, Anna Frazier

All rights reserved. This book or any portion thereof may not be reproduced or used in any manner whatsoever without the author's express written permission, except for the use of quotations in a book review.

Names have been changed to protect the identities of those who have been written of in this publication.

Illustrations by Anna Frazier.

Poems
Published 2021
Edited with Sam Vilicic

violet afternoon

also by anna frazier

Elizabeth Young: The Mind's Mess (2020)
The Moon Reaches For Me (2020)
Thank You For The Flowers (2021)

View other collections at annafrazierpoetry.com.

violet afternoon

anna frazier

connect

Visit annafrazierpoetry.com to subscribe to email updates on her new collections, view featured poems, and learn more about the author.

note from the author

These books are meant to be read in order as well as from left to right. Welcome to a new space.

preface

this book is comprised of three-line poems. the contents were inspired by the japanese haiku, which translates to "light verse." unlike the traditional haiku, *violet afternoon*'s poems are all connected by a few words. each opening line takes words from the previous poem's last line. every poem is to be read and understood individually, but can also be combined with other haikus that may be present on the same page. in addition, lines presented on a titled page are meant to be read in combination with each other. this book does not have a specific plot line to follow, so please allow your mind to interpret its words however it wishes.

— Anna

about illustrations

all of my illustrations are hand-drawn. i read each page to myself and drew whatever that page made me feel. i hope this artistic decision will add another way to ponder.

— Anna

dedication

Within the shadow
I am weaving the pattern
Of a spider web.

> — Lewis Grandison Alexander,
> "Japanese Hokku,"
> 1925

introduction

And only where the forest fires have sped,
  Scorching relentlessly the cool north lands,
A sweet wild flower lifts its purple head,
And, like some gentle spirit sorrow-fed,
  It hides the scars with almost human hands.
And only to the heart that knows of grief,
  Of desolating fire, of human pain,
There comes some purifying sweet belief,
Some fellow-feeling beautiful, if brief.
  And life revives, and blossoms once again.

— Emily Pauline Johnson,
"Fire-Flowers,"
1903

contents

1   self-portrait of the in-between
16   a girl watches a pesticide man
37   log cabin
39   oranges
41   driving through ruby canyon
53   hello i felt loved yesterday
56   black has many shades
57   the fifteenth square
58   low blood sugar
64   list of ten unnoticed items
74   un baiser parfait
79   mars
83   a list of words that intrigued me today
87   explaining synesthesia
90   my favorite day
124   scott
163   sleeping beauty
164   fate of compassion

173   notes
174   index

self-portrait of the in-between

i'm a girl who blushes, invisible.
i'm your heart — a magic, glass bubble.

i am a breath of thunder.
i'm a cloud in the sky in summer.

i'm lavender and your ribs stretching.
i'm the opening of your senses. stepping,

i'm a small pause as you turn the corner,
like you almost saw someone you knew.

i'm your favorite sound, my tongue's letters.
i'm a feeling you can never measure.

i'm the red sweater you fell for when
a stranger asked if you loved me. water —

i'm your cheeks blooming into a wild flowerfield.
i'm what tears you apart and what holds you together.

i'm something you can never know deeply enough
when you're drawing circles with your finger.

i'm a raining roof, a throbbing stomach,
a piano descending in scale forever.

i'm the purple that swallowed your eyes for bruises.
i'm invisible ink-dots on your eyelash, a feather.

i'm what no one ever thinks about.
i'm the shadow behind a rainbow.

i sent my daughter out
    to find a rainbow

she never returned

    i return with rainbow hands
to your body
    so layered and open

my body opens for him

like a daffodil
before the spring frost

    what springs up through
  the frost   except chicory
    except possibility

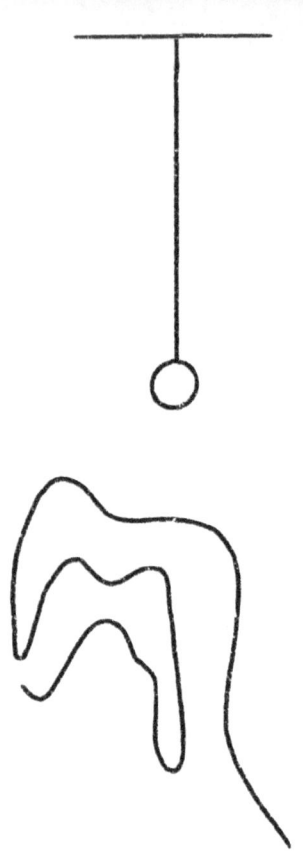

    is it possible   to accept
the way his hands feel
       of sandpaper and pearls

       pearl earrings and gift paper
    are what fold into
       the origami of my center

my eyes center on her
  sea salt hair   she waves
to someone behind me

      someone behind me
  is the shadow   of a mountain
  full of stars   that holds nothing

  the stars hold nothing
from far away   but up close
    they grip a peach sunset glow

    i get a peach from grocery

  consider every poem

      that was written   that will be

you and i were written down

in a book of things that are
living and nonliving   nothing more

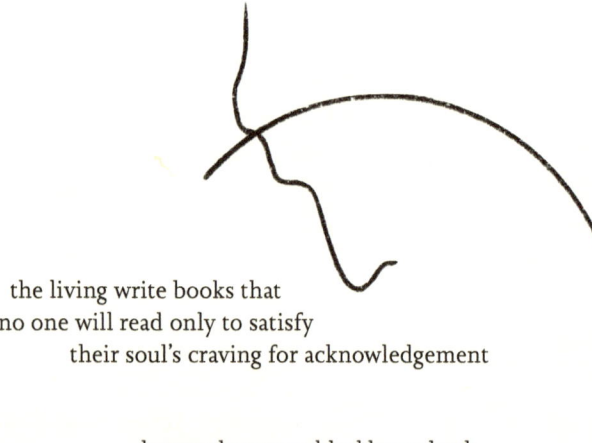

    the living write books that
no one will read only to satisfy
      their soul's craving for acknowledgement

        her soul craves a blackberry bush
  to have and to prune
    under the wan evening moon

one evening i found myself

near and beneath
      a resident pine tree dancing

    a pine tree on eighteenth
  points to all the places i could
dance if i was not under you

      you are underneath a dark umbrella

that keeps out the rain of other
people's love and good thoughts

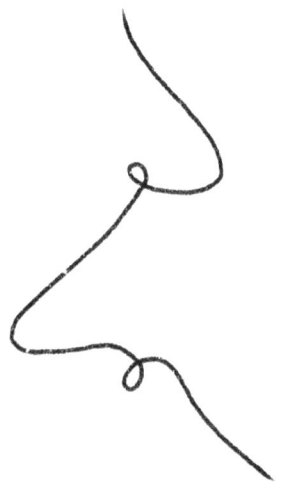

good people are few

i wish i could hop from
        one lily pad to another

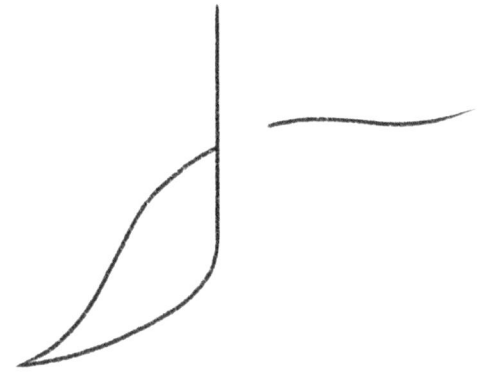

on the bottoms of my other feet
     the skin pads work better

    than the ones i put on today

i put on today   like a threaded sweater
    and it slipped off by
    afternoon

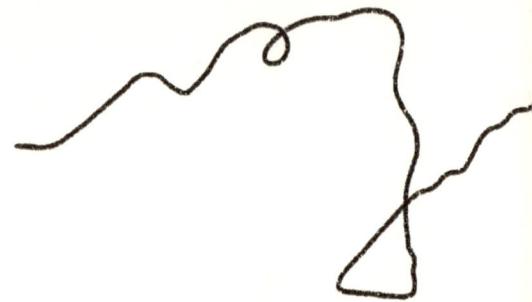

      afternoon flies away like a red balloon

one in the almost-evening time
    i watch it rise in a periwinkle sky

      against the hard sky are
          green oak leaves   is it spring or summer
        what season are we in

                        what season are we in God

                            that i would be lonely
                            for one whole winter

eighty-eight winters and
       one snowflake mountain

this is who i seek to find

"seek and you shall find"
he says   without asking
what other worlds i desire

    in another world with moonlit plains
  a pocket mouse turns a corner
  petals unstick from their day sleep into a bloom

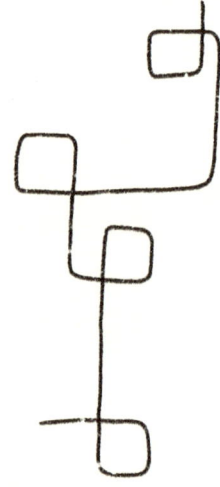

  my hands are petals
  with firm fingers of a juniper
    where can i find this in you

  where can i find you   colored
  aspen of my mind's creation
      sunset rests a long day on ocean's shoulders

  where the desert meets   the cool pacific
  and the teal curve of the crescent moon
      brightness fades for someone new

i imagine a new world where
        all mornings are as glowing as
my green childhood home

        the green wondering eye of a mustard toucan

  reminds me how you fell in love with a girl
  just so she could fill her thoughts with you

you filled me with illusions

a butterfly claps with all her strength
but silence flies out of her sapphire wings

a girl watches a pesticide man

nine yellow butterflies surround a sycamore tree.
yellow scales dazzle & disappear, disappear & dazzle.
a girl squints at them from below the yellow tree,
and her lips crinkle.

six yellow butterflies surround the sycamore tree.
yellow footsteps from a yellow man come closer,
crushing sunshine into the mud.
the girl hides behind a gravestone, 1904.

yellow sprays yellow leaves,
and the pesticide man moves to an adjacent tree.
three yellow butterflies surround the sycamore.
the girl shuts her eyes.

she digs a grass-hole with her fingers
and places yellow in it —
yellow scales that do not shine.
no yellow butterflies surround the sycamore tree.

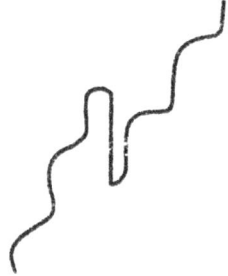

    if i have wings   i'll fly to japan
to be soaked in cherry blossoms
       and hope their serenity washes me

 wash me with warm gazes
splash away my pessimism
      and every man's mistake

        every man's mistake is so simple
     their shallow waters are full of vivid color
  but their depths hold harlequin selves

deep in saint james forest
you can find lemons   in drops
on trees   that wish for ruby leaves

                      ruby wrists dangle over a rock formation
                one hundred pages fall   over the edge

        laughter in a waterfall plummets to the bottom

                water falls in dots over a plum tree

    salt   flats   and   soda   lakes
    paint white flamingos pink

i paint a white ghost   flower

    i'm a bite-sized mouthful

    cold cream that sends blushes up

on pumpkin island   cold dawn
brushes   the shoreline up and back

blowing bubbles that lather each seashell

i blow a dandelion puff into a draft

my throat is dry   i thirst for those light
        seeds to caress a face that i can't

        today the flat mountain is a face
    of spilled rainbows   the impossibility
        of holding color forces my eyes to the sun

        how come the sun and its split shades
        can reach down to touch your nectarine skin
and i'm imprisoned by a distance unbridgeable

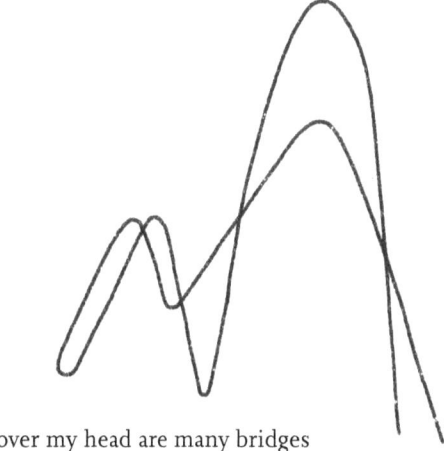

over my head are many bridges

every way life could go crosses over my sight

                    so many sadnesses that i am blind

she is blind to red   to orange

snowflake garlands line her back   when

she runs   only a fossilized breath remains

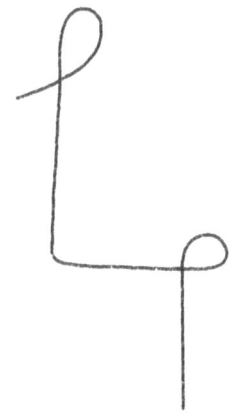

life goes by in breaths
down and   up a chain of prayers
wanting peace

    what is peace
    a day moon
    an empty season

        empty my heart so there's no love
    for him   let me be
    like the pale aspen in winter

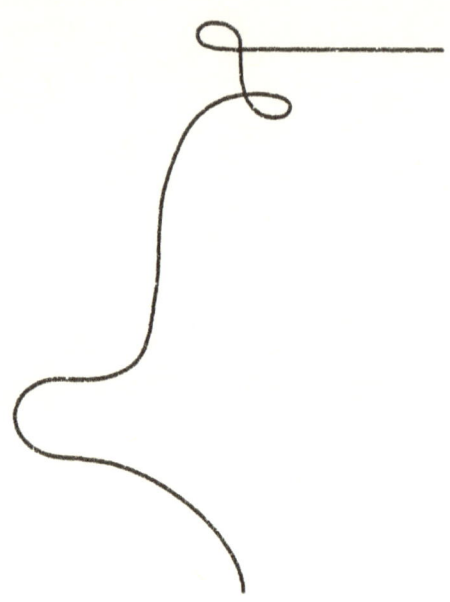

    the aspen and its winking eye
the taper of a mountain tree

one kiss is all it takes

    one kiss turns into a thousand
  one violet turns to three
well at least we have violets

    when someone doesn't love you well

  can a breath be understood
can a lotus flower be wrapped up and sent

a lotus flower on a lily pad
sits content on the water's surface
i met a boy standing by goose pond

by the pond   with blue eyes and pink cheeks
    he's a warm cup of tea   the color lavender
as it floats across the sea

see   he's morning in the valley
soft   calm quiet firm
like shadows that stretch over the moon

        shadows that run off slowly   he's
    how you feel after hearing
       the word "red"   he is longing in a person

God please bring me peace and a person
"you'll understand when you find an ocean"
he said   an ocean of what

an ocean of edge points that all balance
  on top of each other
        on top of springtime and the cold

God sits just next to me in the closet
            we imagine a world where
all afternoons are as bright as my childhood home

  i remember bright scars from irresponsible men
    it's hard to take unshallow breaths
      as vague thoughts surround my body

which body   which lover's cage
will i fly into next
      may i swallow the key

may i be with God in april again
if i take the deepest breath
will he hold it for me

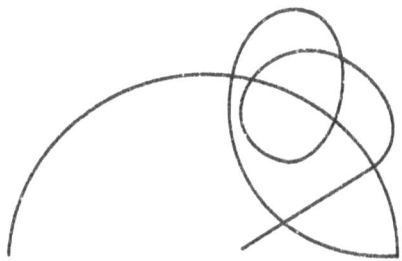

      i speak wearily and am a whole parade

why are you not an entire town
    a toy store with many sounds

i don't let a sound   let you say
       the promise you were almost making

    a kiss   to protect us both

    i kiss your face like the four corners
of the earth   south your lips i always kiss
    first it means the closest we are to each other

is when we're both at rock bottom
    the way you read a book is next
    east from west   one cheek then the other

        one left   north is final
          in the end we are
     the other's north star   a compass

through the stars
you leap quiet and absent

my hands burn for touch

being touched is a middle feeling
because i never know if i'll like it

unless it's the snowfingers of the moon

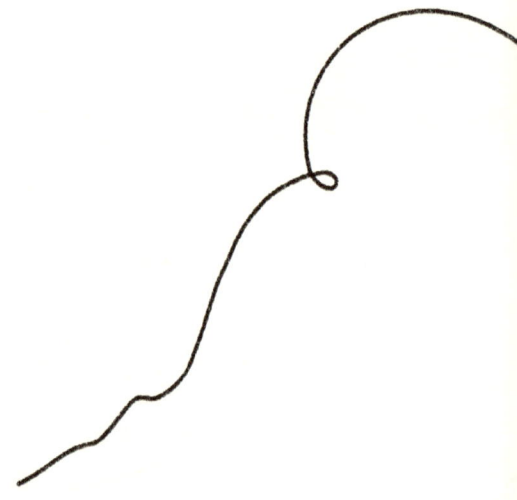

     one moon-shade away   from the color
i've been searching for   all my life
why would God show me that

        God
            who sits above me touching
       my tears of gratitude and fear

     little thread-arms catch my tears
the diagonal carpet holds them up

did he break his own heart or did he have one

           did he have   a tarnished metal exterior and
empty inside   did he use me for oil   slate air tumbles
              around inside his buttoned silver stomach

silver popping bubbles hit
    the ceiling wall of your plastic water bottle

get lost in the rhythm   escape for awhile

the rhythm of   the ringing phone as
     a man on the other end became
          a disappearing act no one came to see

     let's read how he disappeared again
      how he wasn't a home
        and of my own confusion

   my lonely spring is not better than reading that
              after a soulmate   what do i search for
   eventually   the blueberry pie is gone

               i will wander   just as the night
         ends   as the fire is put out
      as the river dries up

         dries all up and then there are just canyons
           and endless moving turns to look around
                  their corners   red

he was   kissing a red rose

a bucket i could fall into

a door that didn't close

log cabin

he says i feel like a log cabin
in the woods   a soft fire   playing
and a warm snow   falling by the window
he says my mind is a garden
that he's been kissing me   for years
he tells me that he knows me   better
than i know myself
he'd like to take what's mine and make it his
it feels like the gentle light   that crashes
over a city   during a summer storm
but when it settles down in the caves
of my vallied heart   it just looks like
something that can't ever stay   alive
do you think it will   *do you think it will*[1]

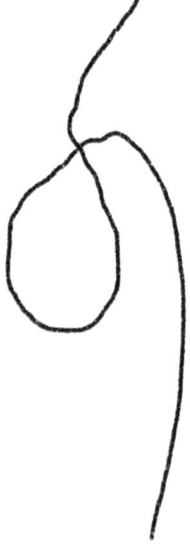

    do you think i'll have a flat stomach
            by the time i reach the door   if i walk
  as fast as i can   all the way home

oranges
in conversation with Ilya Kaminsky's "Marina Tsvetaeva"

i'm a hedge that grows outside of a home
with black and white checkered floors
oranges grow on me and it's just snowed

the dotted orange   the smooth green leaves
and several snowflakes all hanging
in threes on my shoulders   crisp

crisp enough not to melt under a january sun
i picture myself this way so i can see
the whole town and write

i must write in gray heathered balloon   pants
so i can feel the winter air and its freedom
the safety of my waistband keeps me from floating

my olive top floats off
i can't stand the way clothes crawl
on my skin like moth caterpillars

now i ask for more than tanned skin
i want his voice to smell of oranges   someone
who will walk barefoot through the snow with me

through the snow as he has before me
when he was alone   he'll understand that
i'm a sail running near him stopping behind him

behind him i'll think long of his laughter
and he of mine   he will stand with me
on thursday   he'll make cream-cheese biscuits

just because he wanted some   of cream-cheese
and white dresses i dream
about pressing myself against strong skin

about not pressing my ears   closed
while i type   about not waking
up in a warm fuzz   each day

i dream of warm cotton   instead
and the man that warms it
who gets up and puts on a green sweater

he puts on the tea as well and checks
that the thermostat is at sixty-seven
he will like it just a little   colder than me

he will like being my companion
and my lover   and i will trust him like the color
brown   and you will trust him too

driving through ruby canyon

is there someone   a him
that looks at me like the raw topaz sky
calm but commanding   softly overpowering

that makes my eyes sparkle
when i look back up   like the sun

someone that towers over me
like the forest pines
that is gentle and articulated   like the snow

that lands on mountain pathways
that's transparent like the clouds

and can settle into a studded valley with me
someone steadfast   like the rock's solid heart
and someone whose passions spill

out of them like fresh water
in the spring rock formations

she wouldn't trust a spring man in a green sweater

but she would want to   she'd wrap a cloak

around herself and stare at him through the gap

through a garden gap   a bumble bee sings

as my heart desires   but the morning's mouth

swallows my calm

how do i swallow
your little red wagon
coming toward me

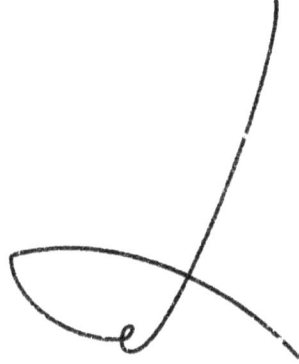

  the sun comes toward me and i know
it would taste like melted butter
       like white hot chocolate if it was drinkable

    you can see colors   left to right
if you glance through your neighbor's fence
     moving   white and yellow

                    moving through its spaces
        a little laughter flies out
even though you can't see behind the white wood

       the springs' clink makes you know
            that whoever's behind the fence
         is being delighted by a simple moment

may we have a moment
for what never was or will be

wet newspaper   everything is gray

he's not everything
but he's company

a house has many sides

i roll down a riverside
between the past and the future
on hesitation's shadow

>	from inside the shadow
>	i sing songs to make a spider's web
>	that won't see the glittering sun

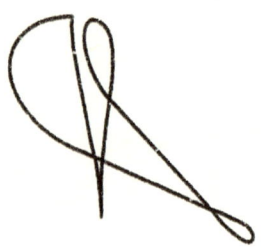

see the peach sun

a snowshoe hare does not question more

don't bother looking down

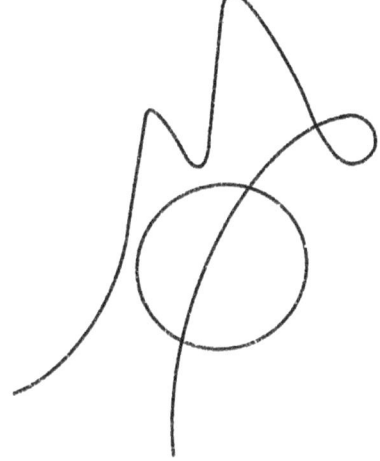

daydreams in his hands
fog in the sugarloaf corridor

come to tomorrow with me

all good things come to an end
i have not seen myself in several days
loving him was shoes too big

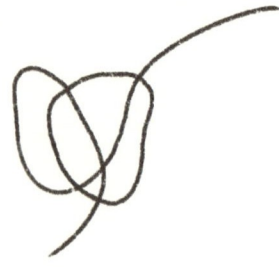

i fell hard for what   just rode in off the plains
he is a sweet cranberry blossom
an arm full of yellow flowers

yellow candied oranges   he's a small town
that you wish you had one more night in
he's simple and warm

warm tomato soup
he's not velvet   he's cashmere
he is looking out a window with dazzling eyes

dazzling more than the city lights he watches
he makes me like the limit forty-five
because it means i'm getting closer

closer like putting a mirror into a sewing thread
and fastening all the houses together
a piano song that skips a key

give me the key that lets me
lay in the flatirons with him
and ride the mountains of his voice

hello i felt loved yesterday

hello i felt loved yesterday
i wanted you to know
i laughed into cold air until it was warm
i went to put your hand on my heart but
it was already there   my mouth opened
to pull words from the sky
but before i knew which ones   you
placed them in that empty space
and shut my lips   my eyes
caught a hexagoned snowflake
i pointed and saw you looking first
"take something beautiful"
you said "how do you see yourself in it"
yesterday i felt close
to you and it seemed to be alright

      i wrap you in the wide ribbon of my voice
          it grows all around you
          like my mother's red tulips

my mother's tulips roll down a hill
  a long road without a turn
you come back again

leaning backwards off my tongue
        your color orange down my throat
   rests at the bottom of my stomach

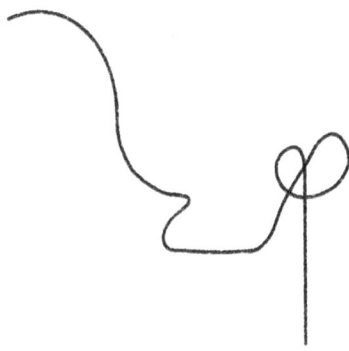

the bottom line is   a kiss and a compromise
there isn't a safe pair of knives
only half-baked people   and someone you love

    someone i love that barely exists
    he put one over on me
        then another

black has many shades

sometimes i feel i am just light enough
not to crush the snow
i don't understand his love
i would so much like to weave a quilt
of a man that might cover up these open wounds
love is pain   survival is often black
love is survival   black has many shades

the fifteenth square

then i go for a walk on a shaded street
i look for him as i try not to step
on little wooden beams

on beams of light i run   there are neon wisps
in my eyes as the ground bounces in front of me
i turn left past a dried weed   it's a fragment

left by the neighbor's fence
i want to see the blue man again
i try to make two footprints in every square

i make a right at the fifteenth square
after a rattling sound catches my ear
he isn't there

there   after a lurch for the blue man
my hope slumps down into a bucket
but rises for a moment

my eyebrow rises above the bucket's top edge
at a bearded shadow on my left
but again sinks beneath the line

the lines in my eyes begin to leap
as i turn to walk away   the man on
my favorite street does not wear blue stripes today

low blood sugar

there is a man.
there is a man on the street.
the man on the street is a shade of yellow
you won't find,
like someone dropped a dandelion in sand-dust
then mashed the flower into a stretching fabric
that the man now wears.
the man turns into a smile.
the man turns around to head off.

i find unfortunate markings
on the dandelion-leather
of his back as he walks away.
he walks along the line of my future path.
i accelerate my footsteps to examine him closer.
i find a brown, splayed scar that reminds me
of a dog's tail in a photograph,
and no one told him to stop wagging it.
i see a rainbow with two colors:
they are his winter and summer tan,
and they run across his arms like
racing cars, like my hands dream of doing.

he turns around, bending down to pick up a dollar
he's dropped, then rises like a stone might
after being properly skipped.
his eyes stay in the air with mine.
along his collarbone is drawn a rusted crease
where his shirt might be if he had one.

i write a poem quickly in my head,

> *your eyes are a summer blanket / a lily pad*
> *floats down a quiet river / there*
> *is a purple flower sleeping on it / when*
> *you look at me, you see behind my eyes /*
> *a silent wind brushes the lily pad along*

so i can get my winged words out of the way
in order that a conversation might begin.

i wonder why my mouth has all of a sudden
become like a donut still holding its hole.
i remember i did not eat a tangerine
before my walk.

the lines on his collarbone begin to wave at me.
the lines on the pavement begin to wave back.
the dog begins to wag its tail.
"the sparkling valley at night
is like someone poured champagne
on the mountains and it spilled over," i tell him,
before my body lays itself down
in the gray waves, thinking they are a river.
i reach out to grab a nearby cloud.
his skin feels like an italian purse.
he tips me backwards into the river,
and after it all, i'm laying on the cement.

what i really wanted to say was,
"why is it so painful to have something
to say and not be able to say it?"

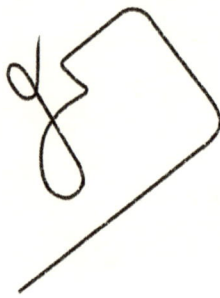

            and i spend my blue prayers

           like a blazing star discards   color
               and dies   without a middle

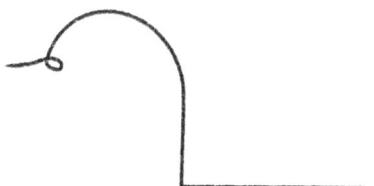

to the middle-day moon

let me rest my head on you

and watch the trilliums sway

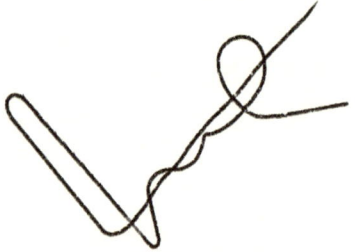

      i watch my body   like a locust's shell
   try to moan at God light enough to float up

and speak to him   but too empty to make a sound

        your favorite sound

                sweetness and light

            a small house in a hidden valley

list of ten unnoticed items

a raindrop's shadow
fallen strands of curled hair
a tissue that you blot your lipstick on
sugar that falls on the counter from a cake donut
a reflection from a crystal vase that holds violets
the person that makes book cloth
the temperature at any golden hour
bacteria on your tv remote
the first drop
whatever's hidden inside a pin-cushion

hidden sea   of a never-seen color

invisible ink-dots   crushed brown pepper

look very closely at the canvas of my woven smile

      than the hungry look of eyes
      there isn't an action more consistent
      you look slow and heavy onto me

heavy weather   slow showers
i'm not heavy on your toes
but i wonder whether you think so

      but then it would be the end
      can you reach for what you've always
      wanted without falling over into it

or over yourself
where you'd be in a place without wanting
more of me

      do you find more of yourself in me
      do i bloom into a wild flowerfield
      when i lay down in you

slowing down slowing down

blackbirds in a waving sheet   in red wearing a yawn

blinking toward you until it's all you see

    i see vermeer's girl reading a letter
        all she sees are daisy waves in the wood
    living in a valley on monarch road

to go on living   what a terrible idea

if i can't eat pancakes made with buttermilk
or see the stars in your eyes

the color in your eyes brightens to a vibrant hue
this weightless feeling is too much to contain
it spills out into a smile

a smile made from autumn wind
from floating on warm air
you hold a universe in your iris

you hold a yellow line on your t-shirt
the yellow line could be a pocket i slip into
i'll focus on the twirls of a dandelion instead

those twirls just before it splays out
in a yellow parade
on the top of its stem

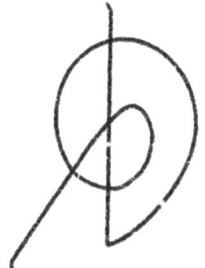

one white flower stem

a brown cow lifts
grass leaves from their burrows

i'm not going to leave   you
alone even when   you tiptoe out
of our room and hope i don't see

    so you can lose hope in isolation
    i'm not going to leave   you alone
    even when   you think it's better

even when   you don't want to bother
    no matter how far into the dark   you hide
i'll always find you   even if

    you don't want any hand on your back
or any water in your throat   i'll sit
as far as you need   but i won't leave you alone

you are a sailing comet
peering at me from the staircase notes
of the song i made for you

between two songs on a soundtrack   the space
where you wait without holding your breath

one other in-between i forgot to mention

show me your bright side   only the sunrise
but i can't ignore what i know
the sun sets each evening

un baiser parfait

my back slopes against an evening wall.
i let my eyes fall on his. he sets one foot on a tile.
another follows, his eyebrows set in a determination
to hold me, cherries in a clafoutis[1]. my knee bends
me lower on the wall, fondu[2]. my heart begins
with little jumps. my stomach leaps and is thrown
up and down. he sets cognac on granite, his motion
toward me a delicate, effortless aplomb[3]. one leg
swings by the other, like a bell's first movement.
his hand unfolds, allongé[4], as it reaches for my chin.
my fingers glissade[5] along his chest-front. he tilts
my face's shadow upward, l'inclinaison[6].
he presses his palm into the curve of my back,
inviting my bend, and sweeps me up in an elevé[7].
my hands wrap around his jawline; we're emboîté[8].

my thumbs brush sun on his cheekbones. he looks
with warm intent into my eyes, une requête[9]. light
from his face drops onto my lips. his lips tip over
onto mine, un baiser[10]. our pinks fold together,
entrechat[11]. my back's cambré[12] forces me further
in; his grasp holds me there, balancé[13]. i taste two shades
of créme[14], absorbée[15]. his head turns, de côté[16].
my tongue makes little circles, chaînés[17]. he presses
a warm mouth on and off mine, chassé[18]. his teeth tug
on my bottom lip; he drinks me. i'm raised
and lowered with the adagio of his breathing, pas de
valse[19]. i elevate to close our encounter, flotte[20],
a soft balloon. our lips part; we look for each other.

my heart quiets to little beats, petite
battements[21]. his hands guide me into him,
l'étreinte[22]. un désir[23]: i am falling open for him.

the perfect kiss

1 custard
2 melted
3 confidence
4 elongating
5 glide
6 the tilt
7 elevation
8 fitted together
9 a request
10 a kiss
11 intertwined
12 arch
13 balanced
14 cream
15 she is absorbed
16 a sideways movement
17 chains
18 chased
19 waltz
20 float
21 little beats
22 the embrace
23 longing

he is mine   and that's all that matters

labels are for   clothing
and he's not   a sweater

he gave me a heavy cotton sweater
when he was in one piece

now it's the only way i feel close to him

close and still far away
a boat on the horizon

this is a pink feeling

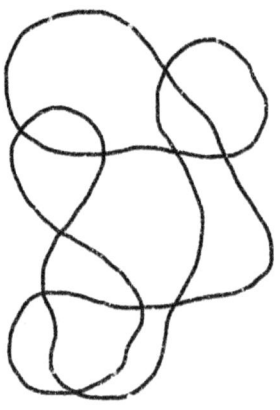

feeling correct   is like a tight hemline
that has no hanging threads

a good way to get around

mars

a pale glisten catches
on my heels   his blue eyes
send me to twist a frozen puddle up

with my shoe-tops   the day freezes
but i keep turning
on standing fallen ice-leaves

i leave to hug him
to hug him is to embrace jupiter
wholesome and a little alien

a little lightweight   twilight zone   rhombus
it feels like the word "maroon" sounds
if you're synesthetic

if violet pauses on a crystal
i pop around on street-ice knowing i could slip
but he makes me fearless

he makes the sky between dusk and night's black
feel tangible   he's not popping fish[2]
but his courage erases the danger i spin on

i spin his glances into gold
his laughter sends me tumbling
into a canyon of my own

even as he drives down bluebell canyon

down and away on my street
i hop from star to star

to star through a wide space
i might bounce off my white rubber shoes
all the way to mars

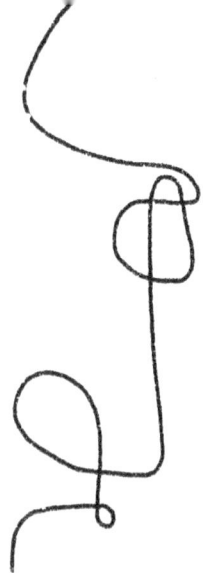

all my energy is rosemary and   eucalyptus
i write down what could fill lavender fields
        with incongruent loves

            loves too soft to stay
            to hold me   that i fall
                right through them

right through the trees   at wonderland stream
four rocks connect   by edge points
in a tower   to salute the clouds

clouds push together   to make velvet
into a person   i will wait to meet him
just as i wait for the last spring   snow to fall

a list of words that intrigued me today

snow catching   cartwheels

oranges   glitter

                                              wind

twenty-four coins half-expecting
                   cosmic

                                            rhythm

   cream glistens   blended

      little finger   blushing

   hanger   emergency   nowhere

       nowhere could be anywhere
a clementine afternoon
              a cream-flowered hillside   listen

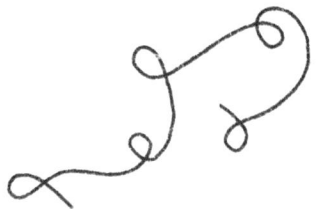

                        listen to the snow
             flying broken through the air

pity its shattered bones

there are bones in my language
put your kaleidoscope on my tongue
you will see another world   a textured rainbow

explaining synesthesia

let's begin with bread.

baked bread can become
breadcrumbs, or mush,
or it can become toast.

"weak"   "meal"   "chaperone"
   "merry"   "teal,"   but not "seal"
      "delivery"   "coming"
              "hike"

aren't the worst, but they're breadcrumbs.

see, all words are bread, which begin as letters — coarse flour. consonant-heavy words are vibrant colors when you speak. they come out like "toast." words that sound like "toast" look like toast if your ear had eyes, and words that are vowel-heavy and also not-french, "areopagus," come out like the bread got milk in it, and now you can't separate the two — mush.

there are masterpieces: "malaise,"
but not as much as "balloon,"
which is about the same as "raindrop."
"punch" isn't as good as "punchy."
"pomegranate," only if the "a" is like
the "a" in "aplomb."

"morning" should stay flat-north-american,
like "boring," "corn," and "store,"
instead of english-tea-and-crackers, "mawneen."

it's been better for me to say "i'm good"
in response to the common question, "how are you,"
because i can hear the letters,
but it's also been worse,
because "well" is grammatically correct.

alphabet criminology
is what i think of when you're talking,
i'm thinking
about whether or not i like the words you're saying
by the way they feel on my skin, whether they're a sin
when they come out of your mouth.
i desire words the same way
you might desire a strawberry or cheesecake.

"cheesecake?"

        cheesecake   is a mouthful of cashmere
then sugar   that tightens my waistband
    if only it could tighten my waist instead

my favorite day

if only today was thursday
because it wouldn't be saturday   an ending
and there wouldn't be anything to dread on friday

friday is like clear water
because i can see what's on the other side
and it won't hurt me

hurt like the color of all the oceans around my wrist
blue was my favorite color   until i learned
the true color of an ocean   black

the truest feeling is no feeling at all
because then at worst   you can just feel bad
for feeling nothing instead of something

something that hurt you
or something that hurts
just because it does

but it doesn't hurt when we're laughing
my favorite laugh is the one that won't stop
with other lovely people

lovely people are few but
my favorite sound is the together-lightness
of "footnote" because it lands like laundry

like laundry in the wind

and doesn't impose on ears the way
a warm tear might if it dropped in

a warm tear might be forgotten on the tongue
but i won't be forgotten today   a favorite feeling
along with being just hungry enough to eat a biscuit

hungry for a future
       i pinned my dreams
like a quilt to the wall

    to the wall i looked each day
    and wondered what they'd turn into
        my eighteenth birthday called

she called me out into the yard
i tried to unpin a few dreams
      to take with me

      but with me   they'd been hanging so long
        when i pulled out their pins
          they dropped

        they dropped to the carpet loops
    like ashes fall back down from a wildfire
        after they've been floating for a time

i float between genres of strength
there's strength to make it through
and strength to ask

for strength after you've emptied yourself
of the first   then there's strength to admit
you don't have either one

and one last   the strength to say exactly
   nothing   which is what i have today
it gives a gray feeling strength

to pull me down and makes me give in
then i await the same fate
as my dreams

i do not glow with the joy of life
no   the churning of my longings
makes nauseous my supine heart

        nausea accompanies me on my walk today
           there's a dog walking
              not without two black ink blotches

      two moroccan tourists ride on his back
at first i think grover   he looks like a grover
has two humps like a camel

    two humps become flat upon closer inspection
grover is simply a dog
with two black spots

        two black spots shift in static noise

                      the crisp of old film reels
             flashing on a screen as tape runs by a light

light that's a shadow
a diamond buried in clouds

love that is not love   waits for you

wait for spring   for the whole hill to bloom

at once   white blossoms will bounce

out of a mountain   and bring you peace

       peace is when God took a palette knife

laid auburn   black   cream down   slid the knife

          rightward over the world and made the gazelle

a striped gazelle   you are privileged
        just to hold a woman's skin in your arms

                    how dare you ask for more

ask   what have i become

a cherry in a bowl popping down and up
gasps for air

         for air in between the magenta waves
         of its own juice wonders
             where the shoreline is

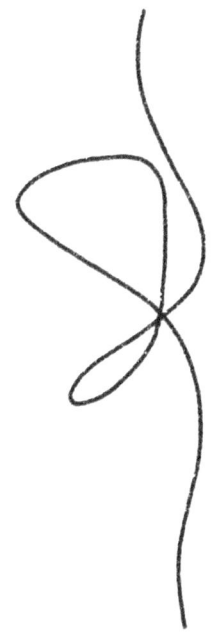

    here's a shoreline where a dozen rings
                have washed up   they now slap
      wet sand-pack on the foot of a gull

     wet drink cans flew through a woman's window
                 to splash the grass   from grass to air
    plastic rings flew   landing as heavy as the breeze

on the heavy heart of a bloated ocean
a gull plus a little more   dives for minnows
   the rings catch on a finger of coral   they all hang

he hung the moon   this isn't a poem to you
     but to me he's the fresh air that caught him when
he was in space   in my lungs   cold and warm

    this space has power   when you speak to me
        i move   when you laugh   i bubble up
        when you cut me   i cry   what am i

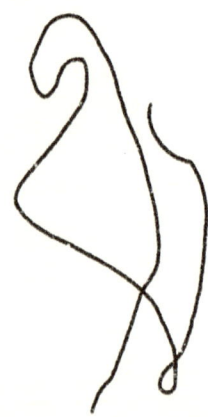

i'm an apple   a part of me rots when you leave
    the brown makes me flimsy   don't unpeel
  a portion of me   unless you plan to hold it closely

      hold me closed   so i don't burst into a cold
sweat   make me warm again like the pale pink
                                    houses

      pale pink houses

   pale pink houses

     pale pink houses

i house a pink pail inside me

my lips puff out to touch cold march air
            will you drink spill kick or lift me

       love me and let me
            cover your eyes so you will love me

    like a desert golden mole soars through sand

      soars   plunges   over under shining granules
               of rock and salt   no granules were harmed
                     in the making of these motions

                    in the making of the universe each day

dawn lifts the stars
from their place on the horizon

                            let us be a place
                                 just as gentle
                      when we look speak touch love

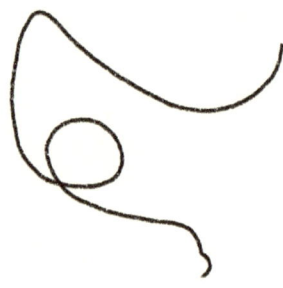

maybe it's the way i used to love the blond boy
                or the face of many men that reminds me
           of that terrible day   in june

 maybe it's the terrible arms of unimportant people
       that call attention to my broken heart
or maybe it's the poem i read today

i read "elegy to my mother's sister"   in the library
        maybe it's the feeling that someone
          is finally acknowledging her existence

     that finally made my blush
turn into a migraine
panic with a hint of loss

a hint of white in all the black
    something only you can see
if you focus your eyes for a second

if you focus your eyes   on her face
you know a woman that collects houses
      houses that sit on her mantle at christmas

      at christmas they light up above her fire
        bright fires   in glowing rooms
      glowing faces with bright commotion

      their faces send a cheery gleam
above stockings   above her
above all the men that she can see

          i collect men bright and tall
          the way she collects houses
              i have them all

i buy vanilla ice cream
sourced from happy farms

i smile with the cows   & none of us are harmed

you feel emptiness

        the way i feel no one

touching my skin   an unplayed piano

touches of a yellow mountain
    then of caution in the wind

    everything that goes up must come down

down on the closet floor
this carpet has a sticking quality

that of caramel or my love for you

you took my love for you   and threw it

when fire leaves a girl
it becomes a handful of wilted tulips

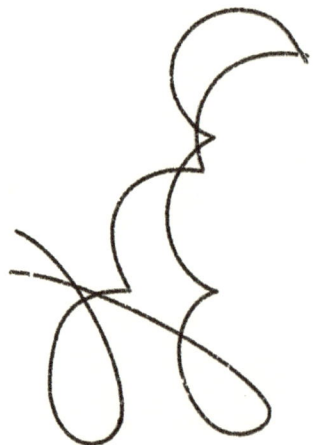

   o   thunder mountain
with thin pearly air   cinnamon is my emotion
        i feel unsafe here

i feel a letter you never wrote me
        like holding a sunrise in my hands
    or a hot soup i shouldn't swallow too soon

           eventually your footsteps faded
       you were a dream that almost came true
               i am a lost pearl in a tide

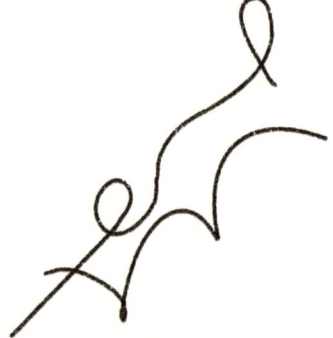

you wish for the world to pause on its axis
to stop for a day　　when at last it does
you ask for the wind

   i hold hands with the wind   with the world
hurrying by the ribbon of a river   arms up and out
       the window   we drive by a meadow

the open arms of an amaranth iris blossom
    how can one afternoon spent in the clouds
    create a desire that stretches to the sea

to the sea animals   umbrella octopus
      pygmy seahorse   arctic seal
        they build homes families bonds too

            why shouldn't they too
            have the right
            to breathe

i watch the universe breathe

imagine my guilt if i spilled a rainbow
much worse than a plate on the kitchen floor

scott

after "Michiko Dead" by Jack Gilbert

i push a box across the floor   just two days before
i met a boy running   his name was scott
i never thought i'd see him again   but then my car
broke down   he picked me up   we drove
to a hardware store   scott asked me to pizza
and a drink   kissed me   walked me home across
nineteenth   i received a call about a dying person
i slept   i woke   scott bought me a sandwich   he
asked me why i looked sad   i had no makeup on
he asked to see the city lights at night   at the top
of long mountain   he told me i have pretty skin
night blinked at us from valley and sky   scott held
me   i held my grief box   he helped me carry
it down the mountain   we didn't drop it   scott
walked me home   we tried to set the box down

      don't tell home about me yet
    i'm still wondering about you
        but i wanted to thank you

           thank you for asking me why
             i like whiskey and
           what makes me a person

what makes me a person varies from day to day
              on tuesday   it was books and migraines
   the next day   it took a turn

    grief turns me
    to a sad woman with a bowed head
      but you notice my other details instead

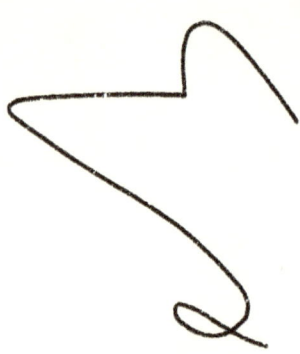

                  noticing me is such a rare event
        for others   most every man notices only himself
but the boy from the park noticed my loose ends

                            he didn't loosen them more
instead he tied the ones i couldn't
        and held me tight to close my wide gaps

   then i could tie those too
the glue of him dried me together
        on into the next day   then he was gone

          when he was gone   i boiled myself
             in hot water like tomatoes
   i mashed my feelings into a thought sauce

  and thought of red pie two nights ago
i thought of "did you notice my largest wound"
and how he said "no"   how we exchanged

the same question backwards and i said
  "no" also   he shared luminous postulations
      like bread with me over the city

     the city where we sleep four hundred and one steps
         apart and where it rained while
           he only saw the good in me

he saw good where i didn't know i had any
        he mentioned ice cream and his jacket
in the same sentence about the cold

        his cold hands were warm to me
            his mellow nature was young enough
            to ask silly questions about dreamy eyes

about confidence and God and anger

    the important things no one will say
while you're in an elevator with them

why don't we encourage each other   in just
the time of an elevator ride that's the real question

grief should not be a taboo

        the real questions are what matter
     ice cream doesn't matter
                        but it can

it can make grief bearable when
     you're walking home with a boy
from the park   anyone can lift the box with you

        even if and especially when they care enough
     to admit there isn't anything they could say
to make it better

       all you have to say   is   "i'd like to escape"
            then i'll be there to hold you
   as damage swirls in your head like kansas

i was glad he was there to hold me

        but when he left for amarillo
                i didn't know who would

she'll dip herself in the clouds
    in an attempt to feel the mountains

the sun is a working mother

the sun is down   i don't know why
   sometimes   i move suddenly
             i call a neurologist   we study my movement

          each time i think
       of the moon
                i move

                              i move on
          to drinks with a strawberry boy   he catches
             my attention unexpectedly

     my attention drifts upward   waxed moon
i remember every lie the moon ever told me
                 i twitch and freeze and wonder

             if the boy sees my injury and wonders why
       my arm juts forward   my eyes shut
with my mouth   i drop what i hold   each time

     my head drops sharply   i look around
to see if he's noticed this quick malfunction
thank goodness i seem invisible

    it's invisible to most   to me it's the world
      stopping on its axis in the worst way
                                  have you ever fallen

                have you ever dreamt and dropped
        from the sky   it's that moment
when sleep jolts you awake

 in a cold fear that you'll soon
reach a death   think of it like that
              if you're awake

           if you jolt   every so often
that same way   this is
my injury   from an abuse of the mind

my injury is a party favor
from a man dressed in evil
who painted the canvas of himself

with my mind   but his painting
is white forever   since each color dissolves
with time

each brush is a person
he just wants art
for his collection

we are not for him   we are not
paintbrushes   we are people
but to him and to us   we are used

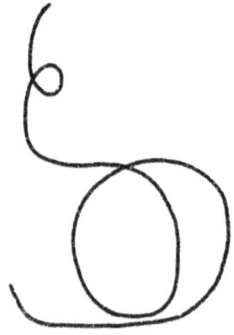

                                          to a mailbox i walk

a hollow sadness accompanies me
& bouncing by with a stoic expression   a bee

      with a stomach paused at the top of its arc
i wait for you   to remember my smile and
   send an origami swan through radio waves[4]

i'd put the radio waves i feel for you
        through a fresh batch   and we'd eat them

        if i could bake cookies without an oven

if you're   the blue danube
                how do you stop your rushing

the danube rolls on over itself forever   grief

      oranges from my bookshelf roll around

they taunt me to do the same but
 i can't spend a smile on anyone except you

missing you   is losing wind
    from my belly

   the turning under of a spring tulip's bulb

      he's a spring berry
    only good
        for a day

good for the day
    you need someone to hold you
        not a moment after

after you're gone
    i ask my prayer to sit
    still by the river

    by the river
we'll wait for God
    to sing at us through tepid air

    a lonely sunflower bends calm air
        under the freckled skin of a tired night
  satellites wave and go   then return

                    you return   & i taste
      the instant pudding   custard of feelings
my heart whips up when she meets a kindred spirit

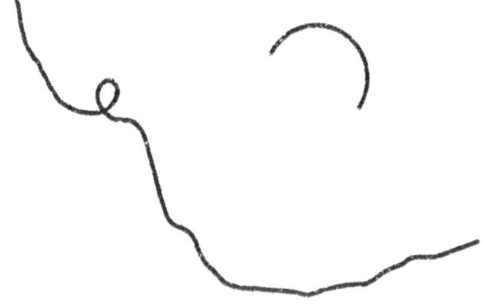

when it's cold   he's company   i want
his sweater   *come back from hidden valley*
come save me from this crush

come　let's share an evening　　　we could ask
　　　for an extra plate and split
　　　　　　the check

check the door   make sure it's locked   check
the time   don't let it fly up and out the window
close that & check my mind   make sure it's open

to hold you in this hour   check your calendar
and push my cheeks into a smile
stay for at least a little while

                                    while i think of you
                    and your saffron hair
    my eyes beam with prasiolite color

           eyes count lights to pass the time   sweep
papers into a pile   happen upon
  a package and open it   only seven minutes by

    someone just has to open it   you can't ask
    a book to be read   neither someone to want you

                            they just have to want to

        i want your warmth
                      drape me with a summer rain
cover me with your quilt of contented longing

forgetting you is lifting my fingerprints from a quilt
or stopping a sailboat
                from toppling over in a hurricane

like us looking over the city
  the crown you've put on my head
 is heavy and still

i'm handed a heavy dining menu
i see "lobster in double sauce"

i wonder if you looked at me and saw a menu

indigo screams at me from the ground
as a rattlesnake hisses
　　in a dark dandelion forest

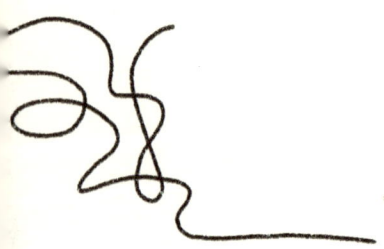

i roll my nose into dark cotton air
and rub it softly into the threads of my cover

so much peace is found before the morning wakes

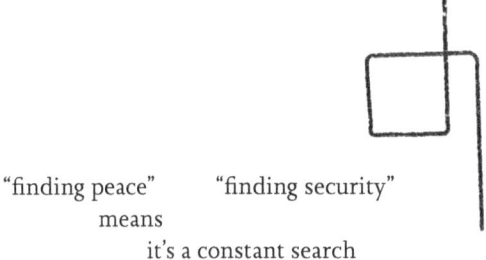

"finding peace"   "finding security"
      means
          it's a constant search

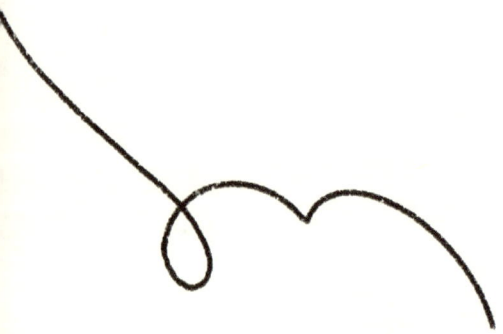

i search for morning   he tells me i'm darling
     while he drips down my throat

is it love

it was love   until it wasn't

don't question the abuse   or her when she says
                     the moon dragged her along

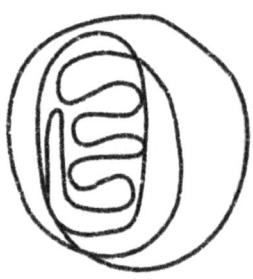

    my ribs dragged along a road where he left me

              he's something unspeakably evil
         a knot that no one should unravel

no one should have to   remember losing
eighteen pounds from confusion   and loving
            someone unknown until the end of time

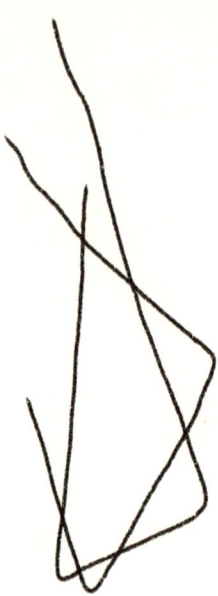

until the end of time i'll wish it was him

to go home to until i remember   he doesn't love
me or anybody or anything

sleeping beauty

i like to think the devil got him
that when satan sent down his legions
the blond haired boy was no match
on that day there was a new moon
his heart turned backwards too
they captured his like he captured mine
and we both fell under evil's spell
this way i don't have to hate him
only the wickedness that possessed him
to do the unspeakable to me
that which was first done to him
may his once-pure heart rest in peace

fate of compassion

a silver sun thaws my garden
while poppyseeds burrow their holes.

i ask the rain to raise them
as dimes drop through peppered rows.

around the corner, an umbrella's hem
brings an invitation — a man.

i duck beneath its yellow panels
and happen upon the stone-gray moon.

a sudden remembrance reveals
his empty face, the voice of a loon.

my chest swells as a blown parachute
and bursting from it, a crimson rage

of lung-skin poppies that open and fall,
letting leave what kept me full: wind

to shut the doors of starless memories.
but on looking down in my blue chest,

a coroner makes her final guess:
"it wasn't love she suppressed;

"the northern lights are not to blame
for bursting wide her knotted seams.

"au contrare — the field of pain
he planted in her has bloomed."

rain washes my blood into the earth.
the moon lights, he even dances,

casting a veil over my white skin.
i'm buried under a silent sun.

i thaw the garden from below
as soft, green stems poke through corn snow.

.

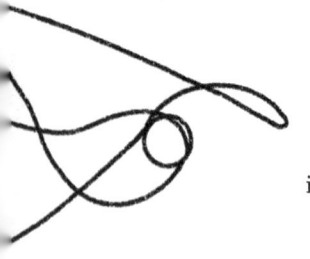

my eyelashes all weep on their own knees

each one blows a different sadness
i keep catching the one about you next to me

        i catch rain in my hand as it brushes my side

            i feel incredibly human today
i miss someone   an empty teapot

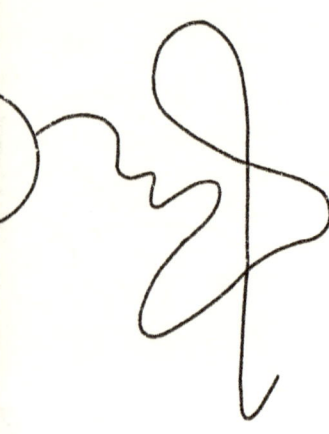

a crushed teapot   now a candle
yields light
      from shattered mud   a cycle

truth recycled my heart into a wandering
                        sailboat[5] and i in turn sorted
      my blue bracelet into gold and fresh diamonds

              peach stones light my way across the pond
          i walk   freely between snow banks[3]
    i forget the mylar and luggage   my hands are free

END

review

Leave a review of this collection on annafrazierpoetry.com in the "contact" section.

Reviews help the author's collection to be viewable by a wider audience, so others can share the experience that you have just had reading the collection.

notes

1. Anna Frazier, *The Moon Reaches For Me*, "Repetition."
2. Anna Frazier, *The Moon Reaches For Me*, "Wood-panel Epiphany."
3. Anna Frazier, *Thank You For The Flowers*, "Facetime."
4. Anna Frazier, *Thank You For The Flowers*, "Red Door."
5. Anna Frazier, *Thank You For The Flowers*, "Violin."

index

self-portrait of the in-between   1
i sent my daughter out to find a rainbow   3
is it possible   to accept   4
my eyes center on her   5
get a peach from grocery   6
you and i were written down   7
the living wrote books that   8
one evening i found myself   9
good people are few   10
on the bottoms of my other feet   11
afternoon flies away like a red balloon   12
eighty-eight winters and one snowflake mountain   13
my hands are petals   14
i imagine a new world where   15
a girl watches a pesticide man   16
if i have wings   i'll fly to japan   17
deep in saint james forest   18
water falls in dots over a plum tree   19
i blow a dandelion puff into a draft   20
over my head are many bridges   21
she is blind to red   to orange   22
life goes by in breaths   23
the aspen and its winking eye   24
a lotus on a lily pad   25
God please bring me peace and a person   26
i speak wearily and am a whole parade   27
i don't let a sound   let you say   28
i kiss your face like the four corners   29
through the stars   30

being touched is a middle feeling　31
one moon-shade away　from the color　32
little tired-arms catch my tears　33
silver popping bubbles hit　34
the rhythm of　the ringing phone as　35
he was　kissing a red rose　36
log cabin　37
do you think i'll have a flat stomach　38
oranges　39
driving through ruby canyon　41
she wouldn't trust a spring man in a green sweater　42
through a garden gap　a bumble bee sings　43
how do i swallow　44
the sun comes toward me　and i know　45
you can see colors　left to right　46
may we have a moment　47
he's not everything　48
i roll down a riverside　49
see the peach sun　50
daydreams in his hands　51
i fell hard for what　just rode in off the plains　52
hello i felt loved yesterday　53
i wrap you in the wide ribbon of my voice　54
the bottom line is　a kiss and a compromise　55
black has many shades　56
the fifteenth square　57
low blood sugar　58
and i spend my blue prayers　60
to the middle-day moon　61
i watch my body　like a locust's shell　62
your favorite sound　63
list of ten unnoticed items　64

hidden sea   of a never-seen color   65
than the hungry look of eyes   66
slowing down slowing down   67
i see vermeer's girl reading a letter   68
to go on living   what a terrible idea   69
the color in your eyes brightens to a vibrant hue   70
one white flower stem   71
i'm not going to leave   you   72
you are a sailing comet   73
un baiser parfait   74
he is mine   and that's all that matters   76
he gave me a heavy cotton sweater   77
feeling correct   78
mars   79
all my energy is rosemary and   eucalyptus   81
right through the trees   at wonderland stream   82
a list of words that intrigued me today   83
nowhere could be anywhere   84
listen to the snow   85
there are bones in my language   86
explaining synesthesia   87
cheesecake   is a mouthful of cashmere   89
my favorite day   90
hungry for a future   92
i float between genres of strength   93
i do not glow with the joy of life   94
nausea accompanies me on my walk today   95
two black spots shift in static noise   96
wait for spring   for the whole hill to bloom   97
peace is when God took a palette knife   98
a striped gazelle you are privileged   99
ask what have i become   100

here is a shoreline where a dozen rings   101
he hung the moon   this isn't a poem to you   102
this space has power   when you speak to me   103
i'm an apple   a part of me rots when you leave   104
hold me closed   so i don't burst into a cold   105
pale pink houses   106
i house a pink pail inside me   107
love me and let me   108
in the making of the universe each day   109
maybe it's the way i used to love the blond boy   110
a hint of white in all the black   111
if you focus your eyes   on her face   112
i buy vanilla ice cream   113
you feel emptiness   114
touches of a yellow mountain   115
down on the closet floor   116
you took my love for you   and threw it   117
o   thunder mountain   118
i feel a letter you never wrote me   119
you wish for the world to pause on its axis   120
i hold hands with the wind   with the world   121
the open arms of an amaranth iris blossom   122
i watch the universe breath   123
scott   124
don't tell home about me yet   125
noticing me is such a rare event   126
when he was gone   i boiled myself   127
he saw good where i didn't know i had any   128
the real questions are what matter   129
all you have to say   is   "i'd like to escape"   130
i was glad he was there to hold me   131
she would dip herself in the clouds   132

the sun is down   i don't know why   133
it's invisible to most   to me it's the world   134
my injury is a party favor   135
to a mailbox   i walk   136
with a stomach paused at the top of its arc   137
i'd put the radio waves i feel for you   138
if you're   the blue danube   139
oranges from my bookshelf roll around   140
missing you   is losing wind   141
he's a spring berry   142
after you're gone   143
a lonely sunflower bends calm air   144
when it's cold   he's company   i want   145
come   let's share an evening   we could ask   146
check the door   make sure it's locked   check   147
while i think of you   148
eyes count lights to pass the time   sweep   149
someone just has to open it   you can't ask   150
i want your warmth   151
forgetting you is lifting my fingerprints from a quilt   152
like us looking over the city   153
i'm handed a heavy dining document   154
indigo screams at me from the ground   155
i roll my nose into dark cotton air   156
"finding peace" "finding security"   157
i search for morning   he tells me i'm darling   158
it was love   until it wasn't   159
my ribs dragged alone a road where he left me   160
no one should have to   remember losing   161
until the end of time i'll wish it was him   162
sleeping beauty   163
fate of compassion   164

my eyelashes all weep on their own knees   166
i catch rain in my hand as it brushes my side   167
a crushed teapot   now a candle   168

www.ingramcontent.com/pod-product-compliance
Lightning Source LLC
LaVergne TN
LVHW041809060526
838201LV00046B/1188